Yi-Hsuan Chelsea Kuo

On Building Chineseness

Yi-Hsuan Chelsea Kuo

On Building Chineseness

Identity formation in Chinese community in the United States

LAP LAMBERT Academic Publishing

Impressum / Imprint

Bibliografische Information der Deutschen Nationalbibliothek: Die Deutsche Nationalbibliothek verzeichnet diese Publikation in der Deutschen Nationalbibliografie; detaillierte bibliografische Daten sind im Internet über http://dnb.d-nb.de abrufbar.

Alle in diesem Buch genannten Marken und Produktnamen unterliegen warenzeichen-, marken- oder patentrechtlichem Schutz bzw. sind Warenzeichen oder eingetragene Warenzeichen der jeweiligen Inhaber. Die Wiedergabe von Marken, Produktnamen, Gebrauchsnamen, Handelsnamen, Warenbezeichnungen u.s.w. in diesem Werk berechtigt auch ohne besondere Kennzeichnung nicht zu der Annahme, dass solche Namen im Sinne der Warenzeichen- und Markenschutzgesetzgebung als frei zu betrachten wären und daher von jedermann benutzt werden dürften.

Bibliographic information published by the Deutsche Nationalbibliothek: The Deutsche Nationalbibliothek lists this publication in the Deutsche Nationalbibliografie; detailed bibliographic data are available in the Internet at http://dnb.d-nb.de.

Any brand names and product names mentioned in this book are subject to trademark, brand or patent protection and are trademarks or registered trademarks of their respective holders. The use of brand names, product names, common names, trade names, product descriptions etc. even without a particular marking in this work is in no way to be construed to mean that such names may be regarded as unrestricted in respect of trademark and brand protection legislation and could thus be used by anyone.

Coverbild / Cover image: www.ingimage.com

Verlag / Publisher:
LAP LAMBERT Academic Publishing
ist ein Imprint der / is a trademark of
OmniScriptum GmbH & Co. KG
Heinrich-Böcking-Str. 6-8, 66121 Saarbrücken, Deutschland / Germany
Email: info@lap-publishing.com

Herstellung: siehe letzte Seite /
Printed at: see last page
ISBN: 978-3-659-58974-4

Table of contents

Introduction

The history of Chinese immigrants in the United States has always been seen from certain fixed points of view. Research on the coolie trade, the buildings of the railways, and digging for gold is abundant, especially research on 19th century Chinese immigrants. The other legacy, of the Chinese students whose numbers have been increasing rapidly during the past two decades, has not been taken as seriously in the history of Chinese American immigration. In other words, scholarship has focus on the lower classes and their immigrant history[1], on issues of discrimination and anti-Chinese movements[2], and on immigration policy and exclusion laws[3]. In brief, Chinese immigration was often viewed through a socio-economic lens[4]. Research on the issue of identity was seldom mentioned in the immigrant context and whom it was, attention was drawn to the way "identity" created a barrier in American host society, primarily through the supposedly "passive" way Chinese were thought to express themselves. These approaches ignored the other half of the legacy that has been built by early Chinese students in America, especially since it emphasized cultural adjustment and identity. These Chinese students in the United States in the early 20th century formed a legacy to some extent separate from other immigrants who were laborers, railway builders in terms of social status, economic condition and other ways of remittance and interactions. In contrast to the general

---

[1] For example, Lynn Pan's Sons of the Yellow Emperor: A History of the Chinese Diaspora. (New York: Kodansha International, 1994.)

[2] For example, Roger Daniel, Asian America: Chinese and Japanese in the United States since 1850. (Seattle: University of Washington Press, 1988.)

[3] For example, Bill Ong Hing's Making and Remaking Asian America Through Immigration Policy, 1850-1900. (Stanford: Stanford University Press, 1993.)

[4] See Christine Dobbin, Asian Entrepreneurial Minorities: Conjoint Communities in the Making of the World-Economy, 1570-1940. (Surrey: Curzon Press Ltd., 1996.), Paul C. P. Siu, Chinese Laundryman: A Study of Social Isolation. (New York: New York University Press, 1987) , Min Zhou, Chinatown: The Socioeconomic Potential of an Urban Enclave. (Philadelphia: Temple University, 1992), and Peter Kwong, Forbidden Workers: Illegal Chinese Immigrants and American Labor. (New York: The New Press, 1997).

stereotype of early Chinese immigrants as being in poor condition, these Chinese students mostly came from wealthy merchant families, and believed in the use of western ideology and Christianity. In the following discussion, it shows that Christianity for Chinese students not only represented a personal belief. Instead, for Chinese in United States, Christianity symbolized other things such as westernization and the possibility of assimilation into the host society.

My interest in Chinese Christian communities is stems from the above reasons. As the largest Chinese association today in terms of its population, the Chinese Christian church is critical to immigration research. The number of Chinese churches in the United States has been increasing rapidly.[5] More than one third of Chinese/ Chinese Americans in the United States today are Christians[6] but in China and Taiwan, they account for only 3% of the population. Most Chinese Christians in the United States converted in America. This phenomenon is quite different from its Korean counterpart in which most Korean Christians in the States were already Christian before they came to the States. Assimilation can not explain everything since most Chinese Christians in the States belong to evangelical are not mainstream liberal churches.[7] At the same time, Korean and Latin Americans also belong to conservative churches as the Chinese do.[8] The relationship between religion and identity becomes an interesting issue to explore in the immigration master narrative.[9]

---

[5] For example, there were only 66 Chinese church in Seattle, by 1994 the number had increased to 700.

[6] Fenggang Yang, "Chinese conversion to evangelical Christianity: The importance of social and cultural context". Sociology of Religion. (Washington: Fall, 1998)

[7] Ibid.

[8] According the research done by Smith-Hefner, in the United States, most post-1965 immigrants from Asia, South and Central America have joined conservative churches. Chinese, Korean, and Southeast Asian immigrants mostly are Evangelical, and Pentecostal Christianity is the mainstream among Latin American immigrants. See Smith Hefner, "Ethnicity and the force of faith: Christian conversion among Khmer refugees", in Anthropological Quarterly 67. Pp. 24-37.

[9] This topic was often treated from a theological or sociological perspective. For example, the Ph.D. dissertation by Fenggan Yang, Religious conversion and identity construction: A Study of a Chinese Christian church in the United States. The Catholic University of America, 1992. See

Yet, the studies of Chinese immigrants' conversion were horizontal analyses without historical context.

Here we explore the identity of Chinese immigrants by examining their Christian organizations and communities from an historical perspective, and fill in some of the missing parts of the earlier immigration story, namely that of the Chinese students, by reviewing their publications in the early 20th century. As the largest Chinese association in the United States (in terms of population), and maybe in European countries as well, the Chinese Christian Church is a pervasive phenomenon that deserves a closer examination.[10] The popularity of Christianity and the active role that the church plays are crucial factors among overseas Chinese.

Christianity has different meanings for Chinese in the United States throughout their long history as American immigrants. The rise of the Chinese church is intertwined with class issues and other factors that are not only matters of belief or religion. Religion plays a variety of roles among Chinese immigrant societies. I will start by analyzing the role of Christianity for the Chinese during the different phases of Chinese immigration history, e.g. the 20th century and the present, and will pay particular attention to the formation of Chinese immigrant identity, and how Christianity contributes to that identity-building. Exploring the role of Christianity for the Chinese during the different phases of Chinese immigration history. I will especially pay attention to the formation of Chinese immigrant identity, and how Christianity contributes to that identity-building. In the end, I will try to explain the meaning behind the transition of Chinese Christians in the United States, and determine what Christianity has meant to them in these different phases.

M.C. Suchman, "Analyzing the determinant of everyday conversion", Sociology Analysis 53S: S15-S33.

[10] There are great numbers of Chinese Churches, Fellowships, and bible study group in many countries in Europe and Russia. For example, there are at least 70 well-organized Chinese Churches in the United Kingdom, and even in places like Portugal, Italy, Spain, Ireland, Austria, Belgium, Luxembourg, and Switzerland in where there are not many Chinese immigrants, there are also Chinese Christian Churches, Fellowships and bible study groups.

Chinese Christian Communities in the Boston Area: An Historical Overview

Changes in the Chinese Christian community are closely related to the master narrative of Chinese history. The organization of Chinese Christian communities reflects the different phases of immigration. Examining such communities in the Boston area allows us to carefully explore the way Chinese Christian communities developed, and see how Christian organizations have developed in these communities and have become the center of social life for Chinese immigrants.

There was no salient Chinese immigrant population in Boston until 1875, when some Chinese moved from the west coast to Boston in an attempt to escape anti-Chinese sentiments in California. At the time, telephone company construction created many working opportunities for the Chinese in Boston[11]. Around the same time, an American missionary movement was trying to reach the Chinese; the first church organization directed toward them in the Boston area was "The City Missionary Society," which was a subordinate organization of the Congregational Church. These missionaries set up English classes and Sunday Schools for Chinese[12]. Following in the footsteps of the Congregational mission, the Baptist Church also set up a Chinese Sunday School in 1893[13], and also sought to instill Christianity by teaching English to these immigrants. Up to this point, the missions were based in Chinatown, and most of their converts were laundrymen, cooks, and waiters. The number of Chinese who joined church activities was very limited. In 1943, the United States revoked the Exclusion Law, and Chinese immigration to the

---

[11] Doris Chu, <u>Chinese in Massachusetts: Their Experiences and Contributions.</u> (Boston: Chinese Culture Institute, 1987), p.6.

[12] <u>Eight-fifth Annual Report of the City Missionary Society.</u> (Boston: City Missionary Society, 1901).

[13] Caril M. Ritchie, "First Baptist Church to Mark Founding of Chinese Sunday School" in <u>Back Bay Ledger.</u> May 7, 1959.

United States began to increase substantially in 1946; five Christian denominations jointly set up the first Chinese Church in Boston's Chinatown.[14]

Another Chinese Church in Boston, the Boston Chinese Evangelical Church, was built in 1961; most of its members had emigrated from Hong Kong after the Communist takeover of China in 1949. Their backgrounds were a bit different from those of members of the other Christian churches and Sunday schools. There were already some professionals in the congregation, although most of the members were drawn from the working class. This church can be viewed as a landmark for Chinese immigrants in transition in terms of the composition of the members and formation of the church, both of which I will discuss in detail later.

The most active organizing factor among Chinese immigrants and students today is Bible study groups. Among these Bible study groups and their antecedent churches, most of the group leaders, preachers and teachers in Sunday school, are Taiwanese. The Church with the greatest Chinese population in Boston today is the "Chinese Bible Church of Greater Boston" which was found by the Taiwanese in 1961. The Taiwanese did not start to immigrate to the United States until 1945 after the surrender of the Japanese. Before that, there were extremely few Taiwanese who could afford to go abroad to study[15]. After 1949, fearful of the Communists and that they might try to "liberate" Taiwan, more and more Taiwanese came to the United States to study or immigrate. In contrast, the Communist party takeover in China prohibited immigration or study abroad. The immigrant flow from China was soon replaced by one from Taiwan. Since the 1950's, most of the immigrants from Taiwan have been professionals who came to the United States to study[16]. Many of the

---

[14] Interviewing Mr. Wang Chung-Shien, a teacher of Chinese Sunday School in Chinese Bible Church of Greater Boston.

[15] Wu-tong Hwang, *Beimeicho Taiwan Qiduqiaohui Kaituoshi.* (A History of the Development of Taiwanese Christian Churches in North America.) (Los Angeles: Taiwanese Christian Church Council of North America), p.1-3.

[16] Ibid.

students, young professionals, and families began to get together regularly to share their feelings and to study the Bible. More than 66% of Chinese churches in the United States today started from Bible study groups.[17] Thus, most of them are nondenominational. The formation of these churches has been different from Chinatown-based ones founded in 1940's and 1950's. The people in the Bible-based congregations came from different neighborhoods. This change reflects the transformation of Chinese immigration during this period. Chinatown had already changed from a ghetto where people had converged due to a common language, to an information-resource center. Chinatown today is more like a tourist attraction with exotic images, cheap and delicious food, services for newer immigrants and economic enclaves for Chinese people in general[18]. Chinese churches in Boston, along with the change of the residential pattern of these immigrants, have been built outside of Chinatown in recent decades; they functioned as providers of information exchanges and cultural comfort. Fellowships based on common residential areas are crucial for this kind of new style church. Today there are twenty-four Chinese fellowships and ten English speaking Christian fellowships under the Chinese Bible Church of Greater Boston. These fellowships are based on geographical locations,[19] ages[20], schools,[21] and are very family oriented in terms of the message they convey; there are also four Chinese fellowships for women based on geographical areas and several family fellowships conducted in both Chinese and English. From this perspective, these Chinese churches represent an "alternative

---

[17] Interview the Senior Pastor of Chinese Bible Church of Greater Boston Chuang, Tsu-Kung. See also Hwang 1986.

[18] Min Zhou, <u>Chinatown: The Socioeconomic Potential of an University of America.</u> (Philadelphia: Temple University, 1992).

[19] For example, Acton Area Fellowship, Alewife Fellowship, Brookline Fellowship, Burlington Fellowship...etc. There are nineteen Fellowships that based on location.

[20] For example, Chen-kwang Fellowship for young parents, She-ching Fellowship for young professionals, Zion Fellowship for elder and the Youth Fellowship in English etc.

[21] For students, their fellowship are all hold in English. For example, Chinese Bible Fellowship on MIT, Inter-College Fellowship.

Chinatown", which provides for a host of services for Chinese immigrants, and they remain an important factor in the network of Chinese churches.

At the beginning, the congregation of the Chinese Church of Greater Boston consisted mainly of Taiwanese. However, since the 1980's, more people from mainland China have joined the congregation after the opening of China under Deng Shaio-ping. Most of these mainland Chinese have been students, visiting scholars, and young professionals with no special religious preference. These new converts were different from those who had emigrated before 1949. Due to the influence of Communist ideology during the cultural revolution and the series of political movements, many of these mainland Chinese never had a chance to learn about Christianity before they came to the United States. As mentioned above, most teachers in Sunday school, Bible study groups, and pastors have been Taiwanese because of historical and cultural factors, but the number of Chinese who came from mainland China in the churches has dramatically increased in recent years. These Chinese have not only participated actively in church activities, but have also "accepted" Christianity more easily than Taiwanese people have in general.[22] The reason relates to a series of movements that have halted belief in traditional deities and folk religions beginning with the May Fourth movement in 1919, and continuing with the cultural revolution and the Communist movement in general in China. After the 1970's, Chinese leaders have lessened the flow of socialist ideology to China's people. Given this ideological vacuum, many Chinese people tended to accept Christianity more easily[23]. For them, Christianity represents the spirit of modernity and democracy behind western civilization.[24]

---

[22] Interview a mission of China Ministries International, Tim Conkling.

[23] Yang Fenggang, "Chinese Conversion to Evangelical Christianity: the Importance of Social and Cultural Context" in Sociology of Religion. Washington: Fall, 1988.

[24] Interviews with people in the Chinese Bible Church of Greater Boston. Also the interview of the witness to the Lu-Gang incident in a broadcast of Chinese Christian Station in the United States.

Taiwan provides a different legacy for the overseas Christian community. Most of the Taiwanese churches[25] in the United States are denominational churches, which is very different from the Chinese Churches in the United States. Among these denominational churches, nearly half are Taiwanese Presbyterian Churches[26]. The large number of Taiwanese Presbyterian Churches in the United States is not simply due to the language comfort the member experience because Taiwanese is spoken in their congregations, although some elder Taiwanese go to the Taiwanese Presbyterian Church because they cannot understand Mandarin. Rather, the reason behind this large Presbyterian congregation is that by joining the Taiwanese Presbyterian Church in the United States, people feel they are maintaining their socio-political concerns and connections with Taiwan,[27] and this reduces their sense of alienation in a foreign country. The Taiwanese Presbyterian church has given people the impression of having close connections with Taiwanese culture and its socio-political issues more so than other churches or over seas' organizations.

The impression that Taiwanese people have of the Taiwanese Presbyterian Church is due to the political history and indigenization of the Presbyterian Church in Taiwan. The work of foreign Christian missionaries in Taiwan has never halted since the Dutch colonial period, even under Japanese colonial rule[28]. So, although the number of Christians in contemporary Taiwan is limited (only 3% of the population), churches have been organized along denominational lines. There are mainly three

---

[25] The term Taiwanese Church here does not depend on the proportion of Taiwanese in the church, but to see if the church stress they are Taiwanese, that is imply that they are different from Chinese, and put the word "Taiwanese" on their church title.

[26] Wu-tong Huang, _Beimeicho Taiwan Qiduqiaohui Kaituoshi._ (A History of the Development of Taiwanese Christian Churches in North America.) (Los Angeles: Taiwanese Christian Church Council of North America), p. 255-260.

[27] Interviewing a student, who live in Cambridge but goes to the Taiwanese Presbyterian Church of Greater Boston in Needham almost every Sunday without going to other closer Chinese Churches around Boston area.

[28] Taiwan Presbyterian Church History Association (ed.). _Taiwan Qiduchanglaoqiaohui Bainneanshi._(The History of Taiwan Presbyterian Church). (Taiwan: Taiwan Presbyterian Church, 1965).

denominational churches in Taiwan: Conciliar churches,[29] Evangelical churches[30] and Pentecostal churches.[31] These three denominations have undergone a long process of contextualization indigenization. The two oldest churches in Taiwan are the Presbyterian Church which entered in 1865[32], and the True Jesus Church, established by three Taiwanese, Paul Wei, :Ling-Shen Chang, and Barnabas Chang. These missionaries were Taiwanese immigrants from Shan-dong province, who were the first Presbyterians and visited Christian organizations in Shanghai and "received the Holy Spirit" and then established the True Jesus Church under the divine instructions of God.[33] The members of these two churches constitute about half of the Taiwanese Protestant community[34] today. These two churches have quite opposite characteristics in terms of their self-image. The Taiwan Presbyterian Church sees itself as associated with a body of Christians worldwide, and as a branch of the Presbyterian Church, while the True Jesus Church actively establishes new churches around the world[35].

The Taiwan Presbyterian Church has a strong ethnic sensibility; in contrast, the True Jesus Church resists any tendency to call itself an ethnic (Taiwanese) Church[36]. The

---

[29] For example, Taiwan Presbyterian church belongs to conciliar churches.

[30] Such as Taiwan Baptist Convention.

[31] Such as the New Testament Church and True Path Church from Hong Kong. (Rubinstein 1994:445).

[32] Wu-tong Hwang, Beimeicho Taiwan Qiduqiaohui Kaituoshi. (A History of the Development of Taiwanese Christian Churches in North America.) (Los Angeles: Taiwanese Christian Church Council of North America), p. 41.

[33] The Homepage of True Jesus Church at www.tjc.org.tw/history.htm.

[34] Presbyterian Church constitute about 36% of the total Protestant community. See Donald MaCall, The Presbyterian Church in Taiwan. (Taipei: PCT General Assembly Office, 1988). The True Jesus Church constitute about 11% of the Protestant population. (See PCT General Assembly Office, 1988.).

[35] Allan J. Swanson, "Contextualization in a Taiwanese Context: Two Contrasting Paradigm" in Lin, Chi-Ping (Peter C. Lin) (ed.), *Chiduchiao yu Chungkuo Bencihua,* (Christianity and its indigenization in China), (Taipei: Yuchokwang Pub., 1980)

[36] Ibid.

Taiwan Presbyterian Church played a unique role in the history of the opposition movement in Taiwan, serving the prophets and leaders of the movement under the authoritarian Kuo-min-tang dominated state (Rubinstein 1996:26). Before 1980, the Taiwan Presbyterian Church also played a role in helping the Han-Taiwanese, the Hakka and the various tribes of aborigines find their own path to ethnic pride.[37]

In summary, we can conclude that there were three phases in the foundation of the Chinese Christian community in Boston. In the 19th century, Chinese Christian communities were based in Chinatown along with the majority of the Chinese population, and were a part of the American church. Since the mid-20th century, Chinese churches began to be built up with the support of American denominations. After 1960, Chinese churches in the United States entered a new phase in that most were founded independently. Although Taiwanese Churches are primarily denominational, given their different historical contexts, they also have tended to begin with Bible study groups founded by students or families who joined certain denominations later.[38] In sum, Chinese Churches in the United States have changed from denominational to nondenominational churches, and from Chinatown-based churches to suburban ones. They have also changed in terms of their members' occupations and the purposes for which they go to church. The congregations of the churches founded after the 1960's consist mostly of professionals or those from the higher classes, while the first Chinese churches often drew their congregations from those in the lower/various socio-economic levels.

The reasons why the Chinese go to church have also changed over the past 150 years. In the past, American churches attracted immigrants to their Sunday schools by providing English classes in addition to teaching the Bible. Today, many parents

---

[37] Murray A. Rubinstein, "The New Testament Church and the Taiwanese Protestant Community" in The Other Taiwan: 1945 to the Present. (New York: M. E. Sharpe Inc., 1996), p.26. See also documents in the Taiwan Presbyterian Church website: document.pct.org.tw.

[38] Some Churches join a domination because of funding, for example, the Boston Taiwanese Christian Church joined the Reformed Church because of the financial constraints.

send their children to church, especially Chinese Christian churches, because of the Chinese classes offered in these churches. Chinese Churches also provide certain Chinese values in their sermons which many parents believe might reduce the tensions of the generation gap arising from immigration.[39] Churches also often provide parenting classes, pre-marital classes and other family-oriented classes. For many parents, one of the critical reasons for the children to go to Chinese Church is to make sure they meet the "right people" for marriage. Many parents still want their children to marry within their race, and the Chinese church is the perfect place to meet.

The rise of the Chinese Christian Church is intertwined with class issues, political movements, and other factors that are not only matters of belief or religion. The pattern seen in the genesis of the Chinese Church can also be seen in other immigrant ethnic churches, i.e. the Korean and Latin American churches. However there are unique parts of the Chinese Church in the United States that contrast with its Korean counterpart. First, the Koreans began to immigrate to the United States following WW1, so Korean immigration history is almost one hundred years shorter than Chinese immigration history. Second, most Korean Christians in the United States were already Christians before they came to the United States, while most Chinese Christians converted in the United States. Third, almost all Korean churches in the United States are denominational, whereas Chinese churches in the United States are nondenominational. In other words, Korean Christian churches in the United States were planed in advance and built systematically by the immigrants, and were to certain degree, directly "transplanted" from Korea. In contrast, the development of the Chinese Christian church is more the result of a positive interaction under the influence of immigration which may reflect more clearly the different qualities of the immigration group, such as ethnic interactions (Taiwanese, Taiwanese Mainlander, Chinese), class differentiation (working class vs.

---

[39] Interviews with several parents in the Chinese Church of Greater Boston.

professionals), and identity preferences (Taiwanese churches vs. Chinese church). The Chinese churches did not decline along with assimilation to American society. The increasing number of American-born Chinese has not brought about the vanishing of the Chinese church, but instead has resulted in the growth of an English-speaking congregation in Chinese churches. I will next analyze the conversion of the first generation Boston Chinese immigrants and the identities of the second, or even third and fourth generation Chinese immigrants who attend Chinese churches today instead of their neighborhood churches.

Ideologies Behind the Religion: "Chinese Christian Student"

According to the records of the American Christian missionary organization[40] and its scholarships, there were very few Chinese Christians in the 19th and early 20th centuries. But if we broaden our view from the Chinatown Chinese, we find there are many more Chinese Christians at the United States at the beginning of the 20th century. Among Chinese students, many of them were Christians. They were very organized in the universities and had very active exchanges. The magazine The Chinese Christian Student, founded in 1909, recorded well their way of thinking and their activities at the time.

The Chinese Christian Student was sent free to all Chinese college students in the U.S. and to regular contributors. It was published by the Chinese Christian Students' Association[41] which was founded in 1909 by a small group of Chinese students,[42] and was only published during the school year from October to April.[43] The Chinese Christian Students' Association asserts that it serves three purposes: the first is to organize all Chinese students into cooperative efforts toward developing a strong Christian character; the second is to render services and to help the Chinese students in America whenever possible, and the third is to promote mutual understanding and friendship between the American and the Chinese people.[44] The content of The Chinese Christian Student can be divided basically into three parts: much commentary on the news happening in China; some current events and activities

---

[40] For example, annual report of the city missionary society.

[41] According to The Chinese Christian Student, "Chinese Student' Association is composed of local chapters set in different college campuses throughout the United States and Canada. All chapters fall under three main headings, the Eastern, Mid-Western, and Western departments. Each is headed by a regional staff elected by the students in that region. The over-all committee is the Central Executive Board chosen from officers of the three departments."

[42] See the bottom page of The Chinese Christian Student.

[43] In The Chinese Christian Student, no author, Vol. 23 No.2 (New York City: November 1931), p.2.

[44] Ibid.

among Chinese students in the United States such as meetings arranged by Chinese Students' Association, financial statements of that Association; and the latest news of members such as their marriages or movements and information about people in China. Commentaries in the magazines were mostly written by Chinese professors, scholars, church or missionary leaders at both American and Chinese Universities, American politicians, or by celebrities who were former Chinese students in the United States; for example, there were many articles by Hu Shi.[45] The fact that there are mostly Chinese commentaries and rarely just simple news reports might reflect the close relationship these Chinese students had with China and that they remained in close contact by other means and were highly concerned about China. The latest news of members (Chinese students) and contributors (most of whom still lived in China), and events they were concerned about which happened in China, reflect their background and connections to their homeland. I now will explore these issues by examining a volume of The Chinese Christian Student.

The first volume that was kept in the Harvard-Yenching Library is Vol. 23 No. 2 published in November 1931. It has a special supplement on Manchuria which was responding to the Japanese invasion at the time. The student authors display a strong sense of responsibility which they share with the traditional literati/ intellectuals' culture in their discourse. A column entitled "Chinese Students Promise to Service Their Country"[46] reports, in referring to the Japanese invasion, that a National Affairs committee chairman of the Chinese Students' Club stated that "… we, the members of the Chinese Students' Club at Michigan, are offering our services to our country. We hope that the United States will take a lead…."[47] In the Manchuria

---

[45] For example, "My Student Days in America" in The Chinese Christian Student Volume XXV No. 7 (New York City: May-June, 1934) by Hu Shi. "China Christian Colleges and American Friends" written in his term Chinese Ambassador to the United States in The Chinese Christian Student Volume XXX No.4 (New York City: Febuary-March, 1940).

[46] In The Chinese Christian Student, no author, Vol. 23 No.2 (New York City: November 1931), p.2.

[47] Ibid., p. 5.

supplement, the column is also basically a report of the Japanese invasion of Manchuria, but written with an angry tone seeking justice. A great part of the mentality of the magazine was inherited from the May Fourth Movement which had as its primary objective a strong nation, and it reveals the May Fourth spirit of the pursuit of knowledge and truth between the lines. Dr. C.Y. Cheng, a moderator of the Churches of Christ wrote an article, "The Church in China's Rebirth" in which he describes the severe opposition that the Christian Church in China had been facing in the previous seven or eight years with its encounters with New Thought, nationalism, communism, anti-Christian agitation and strained international relations.[48] In this article presented at the world "Y" Conference in Cleveland,[49] he begins by stating that "the greatest hope with China lies with the people", and argues that only a real awakening among the common people of China can achieve a strong nation, not the efforts of political leaders. Then, depicting the efforts of the Mass Education Movement under the Chinese Christian leader, Dr. James Yen in North China, he illustrates that the Christian Church was "not slow to realize the need" of China all meaning of the contemporary slogan "go to the people." Basically, on the one hand, he is making the point that Christianity is beneficial to China's modernization; on the other hand, he accepts and is reconciled to the value of those movements which resulted in what he called "spiritual depression" in China. He mentioned Hu Shi, one of the leaders in the New Thought Movement of China as one who "has no sympathy with the Christian religion with utmost frankness and fairness of mind."[50] The author quoted the words of Hu Shi, " I do not believe in God, I do not believe in immortality, but you do. Stick on what you believe. Don't try to water down your conviction to please others" and the author said that "He (Hu Shi) would honor us more if we stick to our convictions". These Christian writers tried to put their belief into the framework of the existing Chinese intellectual

---

[48] Ibid., p. 5 and 8.

[49] Ibid., p. 5. The "Y" Conference might refer to the world Y. M. C. A. Conference.

[50] Ibid., p. 8.

discourse. These intellectuals still inherit the values of the May Fourth Movement, but in their discourses, they still maintain the heritage of the traditional Chinese ethic and its value system. In the same article, the author quotes the words of the ancient Chinese sage Mencius: "The people are the foundation of the nation" to illustrate the importance of the people in order to stress how vital the Mass Education movement (initiated by the church) was. This view might not exemplify the May Fourth tradition and its intent, which was to overthrow the Chinese heritage in every aspect. There are two explanations for the use of Chinese traditional culture by students and missionaries: One is that the Chinese intellectuals could not get away from traditional culture after all, especially after coming to a foreign country where they needed to hold on to their traditions; the other is that missionaries needed to link tradition with their religious efforts. This contextualization[51] was necessary to disseminate Christianity in China. Making Christianity more Chinese could reduce the image of Christianity as a "yang-jiao" (foreign religion), and cut off any relationship it might be thought to have with imperialism and transform it into a resource of nationalism. Many Christian writings in China view Christianity as an engine of modernization, which also embodies and is compatible with Chinese culture.[52] In these writings they portrayed Jesus as a revolutionary martyr who wanted to rebuild his society, and asked for the emancipation of Jews;[53] they tried to

---

[51] Contextualization originally is the matter of semiotics. See Lin, Chi-ping, "Chiduchiaocaichungkuo bencihua chibiyaoshingyu keshingshing" (The Necessity and Feasibility of Christianity in China) (Taipei: Yuchokwang Pub., 1990.), p. 109. Contextualization now refers to how Christianity express itself when granted local authority from the beginning. It includes social, political, and economics questions. See Allen J. Swanson, "Contexualization in a Taiwanese Context: Two Contrasting Paradigms". In Ibid., p. 607-608.

[52] For example, Wu, Lei-chuan, Chiduchiao yu Chungkuowenhua (Christianity and Chinese Culture), (Shanghai: Chingnean sheihui shuchu, 1936). The book stress that Christianity is compatible with Chinese culture that it can rejuvenate Chinese culture, and even become a resource to build a stronger nation.

[53] Ibid., p.296.

18

connect these aspects of Jesus with the materialism and socialism that was popular among intellectuals at that time.[54]

In fact, in this Christian magazine, there are few articles about Christianity in terms of its ideology and bible text studies…etc.; in vol. 23, there is only a poem entitled "Pray" by Dr. W. B. LaForce.[55] The kind of articles that occupied most of the layout deal with the current situation in China; for example, the main topics of this issue are "The Church in China's Rebirth," the Manchurian situation, and international relationships, especially the Chinese-American relationship.[56] Other articles provide information about activities of the Chinese Christian Students' Association, such as the financial campaign,[57] committee elections,[58] meetings and conferences.[59] From the information and the "Men and Events" column, we learn that these students come from totally different backgrounds than the immigrants in Chinatown and have different concerns from those less fortunate Chinese. Instead, the Chinese contributors to these journals have frequent interactions with academic institutes in China such as Tsing Hua University, Yenching University and the German-Yenching Institute.[60] These Chinese Students in America also play an influential role

---

[54] Ibid., p.274-289.

[55] In The Chinese Christian Student, no author, Vol. 23 No.2 (New York City: November 1931), p.2.

[56] There is an article "Chinese-American Relations: A Synopsis of Developments of Particular Interest to Chinese Students" in The Chinese Christian Student, no author, Vol. 23 No.2 (New York City: November 1931), p. 4.

[57] "Our Financial Campaign: Miss L. C. Kung, Treasurer, Urges Chinese Students to Cooperate to Research Quota", in The Chinese Christian Student, Vol. 23 No.2 (New York City: November 1931), p. 3.

[58] "New Members Named on Advisory Committee" in The Chinese Christian Student, Vol. 23 No.2 (New York City: November 1931), p. 6.

[59] "Chinese Students in America: Reports of New Officers and Activities from Many Campuses", in The Chinese Christian Student, Vol. 23 No.2 (New York City: November 1931), p. 7.

[60] They reported on the latest presidency of Tsing Hwa University, the plan of establish German-Yenching Institute by Dr. E. von borch, former German Minister to China, for exchange of German and Chinese students and scholars, and the New York's New Christian leader was also a professor of Philosophy in Yenching University. See "Y. C. Mei Named President if Tsing Hwa

among Chinese intellectuals and bring western ideas into China. They want to alienate themselves from political authority and play the role of an independent intelligentsia. The city most frequently mentioned in their magazine is not one in the United States, but Shanghai. Shanghai is the place where many of these students came from,[61] and continued to have interactions and connections with.[62] It also becomes apparent that Shanghai businessmen have very close relationships with these students.[63] For example, these businessmen write a note for The Chinese Christian Student entitled "To Chinese Students in the United States," depicting the Japanese bombardment of Shanghai and the extended Japanese invasion.[64] The Chinese Students in the United States view themselves as having the responsibilities of traditional Chinese literati on the one hand; one the other they care about things related simply to their practical lives. As they raise funds for Chinese flood relief,[65] they discuss the needs of their own children- who are American-born.[66] These two aspects of their lives are juxtaposed. Their strong sense of elitism is also revealed in their critiques and writings (e.g., although this magazine is distributed only among Chinese students and Chinese contributors, it is written in English). What is behind this, I argue, is the spirit of modernity in the May Fourth Movement. Christianity for

University", "German-Yenching Institute is Panned", and "New York's New Christian Leader" in The Chinese Christian Student, Vol. 23 No.2 (New York City: November 1931), p. 5.

[61] See other issues of The Chinese Christian Student.

[62] In the contend, there are many information about things happening in Shanghai, and their member tend to do work in Shanghai...etc. See "Men and Events" in The Chinese Christian Student, Vol. 23 No.2 (New York City: November 1931), p. 9.

[63] The announcement of Shanghai businessmen often put in the front page of the magazine. See The Chinese Student. Vol. XXIII No.5 (New York City: February 10, 1932), p.1, and many students are the sons or daughters of these businessmen.

[64] Yin Son Lee (a leading business man of Shanghai and a director of the Chinese Y. M. C. A., Shanghai Rotary Club, and Sino-Japanese Society of Shanghai), "To the Chinese Students in the United States" in The Chinese Student. Vol. XXIII No.5 (New York City: February 10, 1932), p.1

[65] "Engineers Stage Play For Chinese Flood Relief" in The Chinese Christian Student, Vol. 23 No.2 (New York City: November 1931), p.6.

[66] "Chinese Students in West to Meet: 10 Universities to Discuss Needs of American Born" in The Chinese Christian Student, Vol. 23 No.2 (New York City: November 1931), p.5.

these students represents Western values, and writing in English represents their link to modernity. This value of The Chinese Christian Student represents efforts toward modernization that Chinese intellectuals made, and also represents another legacy of Chinese immigrants in the United States.

Chinese Christian publications in contemporary America are somewhat different from The Chinese Christian Students discussed above. Along with an increase in immigrants, there are now more and more Chinese Christian periodicals in the United States, Canada and other countries.[67] All of them are published in Chinese. Of these many periodicals, I am going to analyze the monthly newspaper Hao-jiao(Bugle) because it is the most widely distributed free publication among Chinese Christian communities[68] in North America, South America, and European[69]. It also contains different perspectives on immigrants lives.[70] Both periodicals (The Chinese Christian Students and Hao-Jiao) are the predominant ones of their time. The intended readers of "Hao-Jiao" are Chinese immigrants from a vast range of backgrounds in terms of class, occupation and origin (people from mainland China, Taiwan, and Hong Kong). The content of Hao-Jiao is very different from the Chinese Christian Students, being less nationalistic, and tening to concern itself more with issues of ordinary life. It focuses more on news that pertains to the United States, explaining how and what Americans think of these news stories and judges mainstream American values from a Christian point of view, which I will give an

---

[67] According the information that can be access through Internet, there are at least seven Chinese Christian periodicals published in the United States. See the web site of Chinese Chrisitian Internet Mission, www.ccim.org/Publishing/index.html.

[68] According to my observation in the churches in Cambridge area, many of them carry "Hao-Jiao" Newspaper for congregation participant.

[69] There are 230,000 copies published each month, including 52,000 published in New York, 25,000 published in Arizona, 27,000 published in San Francisco, and 25,000 published in Toronto, 25,000 in Vancouver, 10,000 in Philadelphia, 13,000 in Texas, 43,000 in European, 8,000 in New England Area, and 5,000 copies in South America. See Hao-Jiao 1999/4.

[70] Some periodicals focus on evangelical issues, and some focus on the testimony of Chinese Christians. Each of them has different characteristic.

example later. In every issue, there are columns about marriages and children being educated; generally it is very family-oriented. In other parts of the newspaper, there are some columns to inculcate Chinese character. More than 80% of the readers of Hao-Jiao are not Christian.[71] Its wide distribution it represents the need for this kind of voice in the Chinese immigrant society. This publication serves a very practical role such as rendering legal services in the newspaper, especially those concerning with immigration law, and family problems regarding solvency. Even when it comes to "going to church," instead of arguing for the grace of Jesus, it tends to encourage people by raising scientific figures indicating that praying or having Christian beliefs is good for one's health,[72] and the children and teenagers who go to church tend not to be seduced by drugs or violence. For them, Christianity is more like a way to solve or avoid problems in their everyday life than purely a religion. Ultimately is seems to be a way for them to hold on to their existing values.[73] Christianity is represented and interpreted differently in their discourse.

---

[71] Information from the web site: www.cchc.org/herald.

[72] Hao Jiao, Volume 11 No. 12, December 1998, (New England)

[73] Most of the Chinese Church are Evangelical Church, because it is more similar and compatible to Chinese value. Fenggang Yang, "Chinese conversion to evangelical Christianity: The importance of social and cultural context". Sociology of Religion. (Washington: Fall, 1998).

"Church-built-Chineseness": Confucian Orthodoxy vs. Evangelical Christianity

Christianity represented modernity, western civilization, and maybe status, to Chinese students in the United States during the early 19th century who inherited the legacy of the May Fourth movement, which promoted Western science and technology. From the publications they left[74], we can know that for them, Christianity represents the ideology behind western civilization; being a Christian implies an ability to access Western/superior culture,[75] and possibly represents their higher class background.[76] In contemporary America, Chinese Christian churches explicitly and implicitly provide psychological support, culture comforts, and other practical needs for immigrants during the transformation of Chinatown from ghetto to economic enclave and with the change in immigrant background.

The conversion of the Chinese to Christianity is not simply a matter of indigenization or contextualization as most missionaries have said, but a process that is born out of an active adoption on the part of the convert. Christianity, like Confucian values, has been actively interpreted by the Chinese throughout history.

My observation of the Chinese Bible Church of Greater Boston confirms this hypothesis. The reasons why many Chinese participate in church activities are various. The first generation immigrants today mostly go to the Chinese

---

[74] The major periodical for Chinese students in the United States in the 20th is <u>The Chinese Christian Students</u>.

[75] Chinese Students are the other legacy for Chinese immigrants. They came to the United States in the early 20th century, and many of them continue stayed in the United States after graduation. Very high proportion of them are Christians, which is very different from the Chinatown immigrants at the same time. (There were very limited Christians in Boston area at the same time, according to <u>Eighty-fifth Annual Report of the City Missionary Society.</u>

[76] The early Chinese Christians students in the United States mostly came from Shanghai wealthy westernized families.

congregation[77]. Many new immigrants come to Chinese churches for help, and these churches have gradually become the first place that immigrants make contact with when they move to a new area or immigrate to the United States. Some people look for the Web page of the local Chinese church and post a message to ask for help in settling down.[78] On the church's information card (which is filled out by people who come the first time) of the Chinese Bible Church of Greater Boston, a question asks "Do you need anyone to help you to settle down?" The church is actively paying attention to new immigrants and wants to help. By going to the Chinese church, the new immigrants can not only receive actual help, but also can build up their social network in a short time. In Sunday School classes and fellowships, people can make friends with similar backgrounds easily.[79] An informal exchange of information for things such as jobs and houses is very often offered in the church. The fellowships also provide social comfort for these immigrants. Many people go to church or join fellowships for social purposes, so they can find people who are from the same country or, at least, speak the same language.[80] Some of them are interested in Christianity because they could not gain access to it when they were in China, so they want to know what Christianity is about.[81] They see the Christian church as a good way to make friends, seek help, and learn more about American culture,[82] namely Christianity.

According to my interviews at the Chinese Bible church of Greater Boston, a great proportion of people go to church mainly for their children. Chinese American

---

[77] In general, there are two congregations in Chinese churches, one conduct in Chinese/Cantonese/Taiwanese, and the other conduct in English. People who go to the Chinese congregation are usually the first generation immigrants, while people who go to the English conduct congregation are usually American-born Chinese.

[78] For example, the webpage of Dayton Chinese Christian Church has a column for people who need to seek assistant to settle down to sign up. See www.immanuel.net/DCCC/

[79] As I argued in previous section, these Chinese churches draws people from certain background.

[80] My interview to the Chinese paticipants in Chinese Bible Churh of Greater Boston.

[81] My interview to several Chinese Harvard graduate students and visiting scholars.

[82] My interview to the Chinese participants in Chinese Bible Church of Greater Boston.

parents encourage their children to go to Chinese church because they believe the message conveyed is family-oriented, which conforms to Chinese values. "Going to a Christian church is good", said a mother, "If they (children) accept the teachings in the Bible, they will know how to be loyal to their parents." On the church's side, the preacher also pays attention to certain messages in the Bible that seem to conflict with Chinese values. For example, when a preacher came to Luke 14:26, "If anyone comes to me without hating his father and mother, wife and children, brothers and sisters, and even his own life, he can not be my disciple," the preacher drew the Chinese idea of *"yi-shaio-tsuo-chung"* (the highest level for filial piety is to transform it in order to devote your life to your nation) to explain why Jesus had said so. "Jesus does not mean that we do not have to be filial to our parents, just like *yi-shaio-tsuo-chung*,...only if you make Jesus the first priority in your life can you know how to be filial to your parents...," said the preacher of the Chinese Bible Church of Greater Boston.[83] By going to church, parents expect that the church with will explicitly convey Christianity and implicitly pass on "Chineseness", namely some selected traditional values to their children. One of my informants said, "If they go to the church, children will learn more about *renqing shihgu* (interpersonal behavior), because church is a place full of *reqingwei* (human feeling)." The former, *reqing,* refers to "social norms and moral obligation," and the latter, *reqing*, means the "basic emotional responses of an individual."[84]

Parents hope to pass these basic Chinese values to the second generation by joining Chinese Christian churches. There are also parents who want their child to connect with American mainstream ideology, and bring their children to the Chinese church for that purpose. A man said that "I do not believe in God, but since living in this Christian country (the United States), I think it is good for my daughter to know a bit of Christianity, so I have my wife to bring her to church kindergarten." Many first generation immigrants hope their children can integrate into mainstream American

---

[83] The sermon of Sunday Worship on 3/11/1998.

society; they think that being a Christian or going to church makes their children "more Americanized". However, even though these parents hope their children go to church in order to access mainstream American society more easily, another main reason why parents encourage their children to go to Chinese church is because they want their children to meet the "right people". Most parents who are first generation immigrants have problems accepting interracial marriages for their children. The Chinese church, then, is a perfect place to ensure that their children's will meet the "right people" to go out with. The ideology that the church promotes, for example, sanctions against pre-marital sex and divorce, also encourages parents to send their children to church.

The above reasons explain why first generation immigrants go to Chinese church, and also the reasons why parents who are first generation immigrants encourage their children to go to Chinese churches. But these reasons can not explain the increasing population of the English congregation in the Chinese Church. Take the Chinese Bible Church of Greater Boston for example; many people in the congregation are third generation, even fourth generation Chinese Americans, who don't even know where their great grand parents originated from in China. These people still go to Chinese church. There are no adjustment problems for these third generation Chinese Americans since they are American-born, and their parents are less concerned about interracial marriages.[85] For these third or fourth generation Chinese Americans, their affiliation with Chinese churches represents not only the need for material benefits, information exchange and a means to assimilate into American culture, but it also represents a search for ethnic belonging. One informant from the Chinese Bible Church of Greater Boston, a volunteer shuttle bus driver who picked up people from the Alwife T station and brought them to the

---

[84] Yunxiang Yan, The Flow of Gifts. (Stanford: Stanford University Press, 1996), p.122.

[85] My interviews with several third generation Chinese Americans. Among 9 of them, 6 said that their parents do not care if their wife/husband are people of other races. 2 said their parents prefer Asians, and 1 said her parents prefer she marry with a Caucasian or Asian.

Chinese Bible Church of Greater Boston in Lexington, who is a fourth generation Chinese American, said, "I am from Massachusetts, I have lived in my house in South Boston since I was born," when I asked him where he was from. "I am not sure where my great grandfather came from in China, but my father told me that they do not speak Mandarin, but a local dialect, I am not sure what dialect that is, maybe a sort of Cantonese...actually, I do not even know my great grandfather, the one who first came to the States or when my great great grandparents came." In our conversation, he stressed several times that he does not know anything about China or Chinese culture "I've never left here my whole life, even to Maine...even my grandfather did not know how to speak Chinese." But when I asked him "how did you come to this Chinese church?" he said: "I've also been to other American churches for Sunday worship, but I like the teachings here more." Another informant who is also a fourth generation Chinese American said to me, "Yes, I can meet more people who have the same background as me, but the main reason for me to come to this Chinese church and the Chinese student fellowship is that I think the Christianity conveyed in Chinese churches is more original, and maybe is more strict and authentic." In the Chinese Bible Church of Greater Boston, the pastor often criticizes the immorality of contemporary American values, saying the problems of American society are due to the decline of Christianity, namely, most Americans just know the teaching of the Bible, but do not follow it.[86] The most widely distributed Christian monthly newspaper among the Chinese, "*Hao-Jiao*" (Bugle), also voices the Chinese Christian perspective of American mainstream Christian values from its Christian point of view. Take "*Hao-Jiao*" Volume #11, Number #10, October, 1998 for example. This issue discusses President Clinton's affair and stresses the sin Clinton has committed, and explains why some Americans think what he has done is not a "big deal" (Chinese Christian Herald Crusades 1998): "In fact, those Americans do not really understand Jesus' teaching."[87] Most Chinese Christians

---

[86] The sermon at Chinese Bible Church of Greater Boston. 8/22/1998

[87] Chinese Christian Herald Crusade, *Hao-Jiao.* (Bugle), Sep/1998

think that although America is a Christian society, most Americans are not "true Christians."[88] These Chinese Christians think "the reason why American society has become so 'chaotic'(*luan*) is because Americans have already lost the essence of Christianity in their society."[89] *Luan*, as a central theme of Confucianism, refers to the disorder of social relations and political affairs[90]. These Chinese immigrants view Christianity as the way to prevent disorder/chaos and achieve the Confucian ideal universe. More than 80% of the readers of "*Hao-Jiao*" are not Christian.[91] Its popularity among Chinese Americans represents their need for this kind of voice in Chinese immigrant society. This publication not only serves a very practical role such as answering questions on legal issues by professional lawyers on the newspaper staff, especially concerning immigration law, family problems, money matters; even when it comes to "going to church," instead of promoting the grace of Jesus, it tends to encourage people by citing scientific figures indicating that "praying or having Christian beliefs is good for one's health"[92], and that children and teenagers who go to church tend not to be seduced by drugs or violence. The church also provides these immigrants with a set of values for them to hold on to. For them, Christianity is more of a vehicle for solving or avoiding problems in their everyday life than an abstract theological and spiritual center. Ultimately is seems to be of a way for them to hold on to their existing values.[93] Christianity is represented and interpreted differently from the mainstream in their discourses.

---

[88] Fenggang Yang, "Chinese Conversion to Evangelical Christianity: the Importance of Social and Cultural Context" in Sociology of Religion. (Washington: Fall, 1998).

[89] The sermon at Chinese Bible Church of Greater Boston. 8/29/1998

[90] James L. Watson, "Off Flesh and Bones: the management of death pollution in Cantonese Society" in Death Ritual in Late Imperial and Modern China. (Ed. by Bloch, M. & Parry J., Cambridge University Press), pp. 155-186.

[91] Information from the web site: www.cchc.org/herald.

[92] Chinese Christian Herald Crusade, *Hao-Jiao*. (Bugle).

[93] Most of the Chinese Church are Evangelical Church, because it is more similar and compatible to Chinese value (Yang 1998).

Thus, the Chinese Churches in the United States have their own ideologies and values, which are different from mainstream American churches in many ways. As I mentioned at the beginning, almost all Chinese churches in the United States are Evangelical churches, not American mainstream liberal churches. The Evangelical Protestant church is a more conservative branch of Christianity which believes that faith in Jesus Christ is the only way for people to get redemption. It focuses more on moral education and family values, instead of issues of social justice, and academically, rationally understanding the bible.[94] The reason why most Chinese churches are Evangelical can not be totally explained by the fact that Evangelical Christian missionaries worked harder to convert the Chinese than liberal churches, although this is part of the reason. What is behind the acceptance of Evangelical Christianity by the Chinese is that first, according to Nancy Ammerman, conservative religions provide a better basis for people to face the impact of modernity[95]. Evangelical Christianity attracts Chinese immigrants by the absoluteness and certainty of its belief system and its provision of solid values. Secondly, Evangelical Christianity is compatible with Confucian orthodoxy in many ways[96]. Confucianism is an orthodoxy for Chinese; although people do not always follow it, when they confront an unfamiliar culture, they reassert their existing values and hope to pass some selected ones down to their American-born children. The emphasis on the value of family, moral education, and the Protestant ethic of "this-worldly asceticism" in Evangelical Christianity creates a common bond with

---

[94] The separation of Evangelical and Liberal Christianity was due to their different responses to the Renaissance which placed a high value of rationality, view highly of people's ration. Liberal Christianity responded to Renaissance by questioning and using rational way to interpret the bible, while Evangelical Christianity stick to what they had believed.

[95] Nancy T. Ammerman, Bible Believers: Fundamentalists in the Modern World. (NJ: Rutgers University Press, 1987), p.7-8.

[96] Fenggang Yang, Religious Conversion and Identity Construction: A Study of a Chinese Christian Church in the United States. (The Catholic University of America, 1992)

Confucianism. Chinese churches have always stressed the compatibility between these two ideologies[97].

This "Confucian-Christianity" provides Chinese Christians with a sense of identity which provides another central orthodoxy for Chinese Americans, even American-born Chinese. These immigrant Chinese Christians in the United States (the first generation immigrants) and Chinese American Christians (the second, third, fourth generations) gradually formed their unique identity through Confucian-Christianity. This "church-built-Chineseness" is shared by Chinese people who come to the Chinese churches.

---

[97] Ibid.

"Consuming Identity": Chinese Orthopraxy vs. Consumption Culture

Confucian-Christianity serves as an orthodoxy for Chinese Christians overseas. By going to church, people announce their unique social contact("we are 'true Christians'") to Americans and their political inclination (the Chinese church has a different political flavor as I mentioned above). This sense of identity is oriented by the Chinese Christian church. In other words, going to church is not just a matter of ideological commitment, but is itself a social interaction. As the Chinese Confucian World is held together by orthopraxy (correct practice) rather than orthodoxy (correct belief)[98], this "Church-oriented-Chineseness" is formed by, rather than results from, people who identify with this "Confucian-Christianity" ideology; but through participating in the Chinese church, people imagine for themselves a certain identity. As I illustrated, the Chinese churches in the Boston area reflect inherited class and political distinctions in their composition. Take the most explicit case for example. A Chinese person attending a Taiwanese Presbyterian Church in the United States is probably someone who might favor Taiwan's independence, and hope to build certain social-political connections to Taiwan. Each church has its own distinct character in terms of its class orientation or political flavor. Today, the factors behind the formation of certain church characteristics may no longer exist, but these characteristics have been resources for people who seek a sense of belonging, as a way of conveying their imagined social status or political opinion. The imagining people engage in by going to church serves a critical role. The Chinese church is a perfect place for this work of imagination. Not only do the specific characteristic of a church provide first generation immigrants with a sense of belonging, but by going to a Chinese church these Chinese Americans confirm their identity by announcing their authentic beliefs. Students, new immigrants, and Chinese Americans of the

---

[98] James L. Watson, "Confucian Models at the Local Level Ideology and Practice in South China" in The Universal and Particular Natures of Confucianism. (Ed. by Bloch, M. & Parry, J.,) (Cambridge University Press), p155-186.

second, third, fourth… generation come to the church to stimulate and exercise their imagination.

These Chinese/Chinese Americans not only consume Christianity for the conventional character that its evangelical form may have, but because it also provides the most practical ideology for their social situation nowadays. As I mentioned in a previous section, the value of family was emphasized in the Chinese church, but these teachings are not identical with the traditional Chinese orthodox ideology; many of the Christian teachings that these Chinese churches stress coincide with the trend toward modern ideas and criticize some traditional Chinese ideology. For example, when the Sunday School teacher spoke of the ideal Christian-like family in the class, she pointed out that its focus should be the husband and wife, not the parents of the husband. "According to the teaching of Bible in Genesis 2:24 and Ephesians 5:31, 'A Man shall leave his father and his mother and be joined to his wife and the two shall become one flesh'. We Chinese used to think of ourselves as a part of our parents' family, for example, living with parents even after marrying, attitudes which might cause some problems." "To leave our parents after getting married does not mean we are not filial to our parents, but means we know how to take responsibility for the new family we built."[99] This teaching coincides with the trend of modern society's family pattern, which is the emergence of a 'conjugal' pattern of family life, namely the husband-wife bond which has become the center of family among Chinese[100], especially among those Chinese in the United States[101]. What I argue here is that the kind of Christianity

---

[99] By the teacher of the Baptism Class in Chinese Bible Church of Greater Boston at 4/18/1999.

[100] Martin King Whyte, "The Fate of Filial Obligation in Urban China" in The China Journal, no.38 (Australian National University Press) pp.1-31. Yunxiang Yan, "The Triumph of Conjugality: Structural Transformation of Family Relations in a Chinese Village" in Ethnology 36 (3) (Summer 97), pp. 191-212.

[101] In the research conducted by Yoshinori Kamo and Min Zhou, they found that the patterns of living arrangement among elderly Chinese persist longer than expected, but indeed have undergo some change under the influence of acculturation. The proportion of three-generation and other extended Chinese family households in the United States is lower than it is in China. See Kamo,

taught in Chinese Churches is a feasible ideology which accommodates with both the traditional background of these Chinese and the modern challenge they are facing. In other words, Christianity is more like a solution than just an ideology. People who attend Chinese churches view this "Christian way of life" as an ideal model, and portray an "authentic Christian life style" in their belief. By participating in Chinese churches, members consume this "Confucian-Christianity" to hold their values together. The take on Christianity for Chinese of "the second universe"[102] is different than for those of "the first universe."[103] For Chinese in the first universe, converting to Christianity is a matter of personal belief or faith, which is mostly unrelated to other family members and seldom influences other family members; however, in the Chinese Churches in the United States, going to church is a family activity, and Christianity for them is not only a personal faith, but is seen as a lifestyle which should be acted out through the interaction of family members, and the renovation of the value system. As a Sunday School teacher pointed out, "It is very precious that most brothers and sisters here in our church come with their wives and husbands. They believe in Jesus together, not necessarily at the same time, but one will soon follow the other." "The situation we have here is quite different from the one that I saw in Taiwan. There it is very common to see a sister in the church whose husband is an atheist, or a brother who comes from a Buddhist family."[104] This difference not only tells us the simple fact that Christianity for Chinese in the United States is more family-oriented. Moreover, it illustrates the different meanings of Christianity for Chinese in their native land and for immigrants. For these members of Chinese Churches, Christianity is more than a religion, belief or faith,

---

Yoshinori and Min Zhou, "Living arrangements of elderly Chinese and Japanese in the United States" in Journal of Marriage and the Family. Vol. 56 Issue 3. (Minneapolis, Aug 1994)

[102] "The second universe" refers to Chinese Community throughout the world. See Wei-Ming Tu, "Cultural China: The Peripheries as the Center" in The Living Tree: The Changing Meaning of Being Chinese Today. (Stanford: Stanford University, 1994), p.13.

[103] "The first universe" refers to societies which consist of predominantly cultural or ethnic Chinese. See Ibid.

[104] A Sunday School teacher mentioned so in the class at 4/18/1999.

but more like an activity, an intermediate ideology that can be shared between family members. From this perspective, going to church can be seen as a consumption behavior. By going to church, people receive ways to solve the problems and deal with the frustrations they encounter. The help that these Chinese Churches render include practical help, psychological consoling, and sense of identity-- the Church-oriented-Chineseness that I mentioned above. "Chineseness" is strengthened when these members consume these features offered by these Churches.

Thus, Christianity is followed by these members in an active way; not only does Christianity provide a belief system closely allow existing values that these Chinese have, but also these members of Chinese churches, to some degree, actively create a sub-culture which holds them together. They do not come to the Chinese church simply to worship Confucian-Christian orthodoxy, but to claim their identity; their sense of uniqueness is provided by Confucian Christianity. Therefore, Chinese Americans are not born with "Chineseness". They come to attain 'Chineseness' by consuming what I call "Confucian Christianity".

Conclusion

Christianity has been interpreted differently in the master narrative of Chinese immigrants. In the early 20th century, Christianity represent modernity and western civilization, and maybe status to Chinese students. In contemporary America, Chinese Christian churches explicitly and implicitly provide psychological and cultural comforts, and other practical needs for immigrants during the transformation of Chinatown from its ghettoized form to an economic enclave, and the related change of immigrant background. By examining the Chinese Christian students in the early 20th century, we can not only supply a missing part of immigration history in the United States, but also came to know the value system behind their conversion. By reviewing the overseas Christian communities historically, I argue that the conversion of Chinese to Christianity is not only a matter of indigenization or contextualization, but a process born out of an active adoption on the part of the converts. Christianity, like other Confucian values, was actively interpreted by Chinese throughout history, and their interpretation reflects a lively master narrative of Chinese history.

Exploring the Christian community in Boston Chinese churches today shows us that Christianity has become an ideology that many Chinese immigrants transform and identify with. This "Christianity with a Chinese character" was achieved by the historical transformation of Chinatown, physiological need, and the practical help that the church has rendered. However, this "Confucian-Christianity" furthermore provides a basis for the formation of Chinese identity. Thus, Chinese Christian churches attract not only first generation immigrants who arrive with the problem of assimilating into mainstream American society, but also draw more and more the second, third, fourth generation Chinese Americans who join the church and share in this identity which is oriented/created by the church.

35

Moreover, "Confucian-Christianity" is the common ideology shared by those Chinese Americans, but it is not the motive for them to go to a Chinese church. The key to activating their identity is the consumption mechanism. Going to church is a reason for many immigrants to display their class, political inclinations, and their uniqueness in American society in general. That is, they do not identify with this "Confucian-Christianity" orthodoxy, but by consuming "Confucian-Christianity", they are able to identify themselves. In other words, it is this practice of consumption that defines a "Church-oriented identity" rather than the ideology of Confucian-Christianity.

Christianity has had different meanings for Chinese in the United States throughout their long history as American immigrants. The rise of the Chinese church is intertwined with class issues and other factors that are not only matters of belief or religion. Religion plays a variety of roles among Chinese immigrant societies. In this long history, Christianity has always to some extent been seen as a symbol, or a mediator to western modernity, but in the process of identity and national building, Christianity has served a different role. For the Chinese Christian student in the early 20th century, Christianity is one of the components of modernity and an ideological base for constructing China as a modern nation-state. Anderson emphasizes the "imagined" nature of nationalism[105]; Christianity exactly serves this function of imagination. For the Chinese Christian community today, Christianity is still a metaphor something else instead of being just a religion or personal belief. I found that conversion to some extent fits the model of a consumption culture during the transformations of the nation-states[106]. The consumption of Christian ideology holds the Chinese identity, that is to say, these Chinese/Chinese American Christians were held together not by Christianity as a religion or ideology, but as an aspect of

---

[105] Benedict Anderson, Imagined Communities: Reflections on the Origin and Spread of Nationalism. (London: Verso, 1983).

[106] Arjun Appadurai, Modernity at Large: Cultural Dimension of Globalization. (Minneapolis: Minnesota Press, 1996).

consumption culture. From this culture they share in the church, they complete their sense of belonging and identity.

Bibliography

Books

Ammerman, Nancy T. *Bible Believers: Fundamentalists in the Modern World.* NJ: Rutgers University Press, 1987.

Anderson, Benedict. *Imagined Communities: Reflections on the Origin and Spread of Nationalism.* London: Verso, 1983.

Appadurai, Arjun. *Modernity at Large: Cultural Dimension of Globalization.* Minneapolis: Minnesota Press, 1996.

Chu, Doris C. J. *Chinese in Massachusetts: Their Experiences and Contributions.* Boston: Chinese Culture Institute, 1987.

Daniel, Roger. *Asian America: Chinese and Japanese in the United States since 1850.* Seattle: University of Washington Press, 1988.

Dobbin, Christian. *Asian Entrepreneurial Minorities: Conjoint Communities in the Making of the World Economy.* Surry: Curzon Press Ltd., 1996.

Hing, Bill Ong. *Making and Remaking Asian America Through Immigration Policy 1950-1900.* Stanford: Stanford University, 1993.

Hwang, Wu-tong. *Beimeicho Taiwan Qiduqiaohui Kaituoshi. (A History of the Development of Taiwanese Christian Churches in North America.)* Los Angeles: Taiwanese Christian Church Council of North America, 1986.

Kwang, Peter. *Forbidden Workers: Illegal Chinese Immigrants and American Labor.* New York: The New Press, 1997.

Lin, Chi-ping (Peter C. Lin) (ed.), *Chiduchiao Yu Chungkuo Bencihua. (Christianity and its indigenization in China),* Taipei: Yuchokwang Pub. ,1980.

MaCall, Donald. *The Presbyterian Church in Taiwan.* Taipei: PCT General Assembly Office, 1988.

Pan, Lin. *Sons of the Yellow Emperor: A History of the Chinese Diaspora.* New York: Kodansha International, 1994.

Siu, Paul C. P.. *Chinese Laundryman: A Study of Social Isolation.* New York: New York University Press, 1987.

Taiwan Presbyterian Church History Association (ed.). *Taiwan Qiduchanglaoqiaohui Baineanshi. (The History of Taiwan Presbyterian Church).* Taiwan: Taiwan Presbyterian Church, 1965.

Wu, Lei-chuan, *Chiduchiao yu Chungkuowenhua_(Christianity and Chinese Culture),* Shanghai: Chingnean sheihui shuchu, 1936.

Yan, Yunxiang. *The Flow of Gifts.* Stanford: Stanford University Press, 1996.

Yang, Fenggang. *Religious Conversion and Identity Construction: A Study of a Chinese Christian Church in the United States.* The Catholic University of America, 1992.

Zhou, Min. *Chinatown: The Socioeconomic Potential of an Urban Enclave.* Philadelphia: Temple University, 1992.

Eighty-fifth Annual Report of the City Missionary Society. Boston: 1901.

Hsintu Taipiao Ta Hui Yi An. Recommendations of the General Convention of the Laity., (Taichung: General Assembly Office, 1988.

Articles

Hefner, Smith. "Ethnicity and the Force of Faith: Christian Conversion among Khmer Refugees" in *Anthropological Quarterly.* 67.

Lin, Chi-ping, *"Chiduchiaocaichungkuo bencihua chibiyaoshingyu keshingshing" (The Necessity and Feasibility of Christianity in China).* Taipei: Yuchokwang Pub., 1990.

Ritchie, Caril M. "First Baptist Church to Mark Founding of Chinese Sunday School" in *Back Bay Ledger.* May 7, 1959.

Rubinstein, Murray A.. "The New Testament Church and the Taiwanese Protestant Communit" in *The Other Taiwan: 1945 to the Present*, ed. by Murray Rubinstein A. New York: M. E. Sharpe Inc.

Rubinstein, Murray A.. "Christianity and Democratization in Modern Taiwan: The Presbyterian Church and the Struggle for Minnan/Hakka Selfhood in the Republic of China" (unpublished).

Suchman, M. C. "Analyzing the determinant of everyday conversion" in *Sociology Analysis.* 53S.

Swanson Allen J. , "Contexualization in a Taiwanese Context: Two Contrasting Paradigm" in *Chiduchiao Yu Chungkuo Bencihua. (Christianity and its indigenization in China)*, ed. by Lin, Chi-ping (Peter C. Lin) , Taipei: Yuchokwang Pub. ,1980.

Tu, Wei-ming, "Cultural China: The Peripheries as the Center". In *The Living Three: The Changing Meanings of Being Chinese Today.* Stanford: Stanford University Press, 1994.

Watson, James L. "Of Flesh and Bones: the management of death pollution in Cantonese Society" in *Death Ritual in Late Imperial and Modern China.* Edited by Bloch, M. & Parry, J.,Cambridge University Press. Pp.155-186, 1982.

Watson, James L. "Confucian Models at the Local Level Ideology and Practice in South China" in *The Universal and Particular Natures of Confucianism*, ed. by Academy of the 8th International Conference in Korean Studies, 1994.

Whyte, Martin K. "The Fate of Filial Obligations in Urban China" in *China Journal.* No.38. Australian National University, pp.1-31.

Yan, Yunxiang. "The Triumph of Conjugality: Structural Transformation of Family Relations in a Chinese Village," in *Ethnology.* 36 (3) (Summer 1997), pp. 191-212.

Yang, Fenggang. "Chinese Conversion to Evangelical Christianity: The Importance of Social and Cultural Context" in *Sociology of Religion.* Washington: Fall, 1988.

Zhou, Min and Kamo, Yoshinori. "Living Arrangements of Elderly Chinese and Japanese in the United States" in *Journal of Marriage and the Family.* Vol.56, Issue 3. Minneapolis: National Council on Family Relations. Aug 1994.

Periodicals and Newspapers

Chinese Christian Student New York: Chinese Students' Christian Association.

Volume 23 No. 2 (November, 1931).

Volume XXV No.7 (May-June, 1934).

Volume XXX No.4 (February-March, 1940).

Hao-Jiao Chinese Christian Herald Crusade.

Vol. 11 No. 10 October 1998.

Vol. 10 No. 12 December 1998.

Web Page

Chinese Christian Internet Mission: http:// www.ccim.org/publishing/index.html

Dayton Chinese Christian Church: http:// www.immanuel.net/DCCC/

Hao Jiao Monthly Newapaper: http:// www.cchc.org/herald

Taiwan Presbyterian Church: http:// www.document.ptc.org.tw

Druck:
Canon Deutschland Business Services GmbH
im Auftrag der KNV-Gruppe
Ferdinand-Jühlke-Str. 7
99095 Erfurt